THINE

THINE

KATE PARTRIDGE

T|P
Tupelo Press
North Adams, Massachusetts

THINE

ISBN-13: 978-1-961209-00-8 (paper); 978-1-961209-04-6 (eBook)
Library of Congress Control Number: 2023940986

Cover and text design by Bill Kuch.

First paperback edition September 2023

Tupelo Press
P.O. Box 1767
North Adams, Massachusetts 01247
(413) 664-9611 / Fax: (413) 664-9711
editor@tupelopress.org / www.tupelopress.org

Tupelo Press is an award-winning independent literary press that publishes fine fiction, non-fiction, and poetry in books that are a joy to hold as well as read. Tupelo Press is a registered 501(c)(3) nonprofit organization, and we rely on public support to carry out our mission of publishing extraordinary work that may be outside the realm of the large commercial publishers. Financial donations are welcome and are tax deductible.

for Lucy

Table of Contents

THREE

ONE

Ode on Inheritance

It begins, as usual, with the narrative of water:
                           a sudden
                  spring on a dark slope,
            the ensuing drape of green. At the base, a kidney
lake

wrinkles in its skin. If this is a metaphor for faith, then
                           it must be
                  impacted by the
            next scene, where a great canyon weighs against cliffs cloaked in
fire,

perhaps a thick rain. I could describe the dense afternoon with
                           the bicycle,
                  the desert, the hail,
            the available tree, the decision: soak or wait.
In

this case, no one did. Would you believe me if I said, as I
                           watched pellets
                  of hail melting in-
            to my shirt, that it changed me? And when, just past the ridge,
I

saw the burn crouching through the valley, when I saw the bore marks
                           driving into
                  the ridges, that was when
            I felt the pockmarked future, the balance shifting from
rock

to air. Remember, the water and its course have long ended.
The hills cling
in silence, while on
their ribs, the assiduous trees sculpt themselves from their
own embers.

Theory of Audacity

California the city always with its beehive hair
over the ridge,
pew pew of birds pinging their locations,
and California houses standing on one foot on the hills
in matching hats
the styles of various revivals.

I have gone out to let things gather around me.

In the Barocci painting, Aeneas stands among things
to be shed as skin:
a wife, the rectangular walls of his home,

the city itself with its empty watchtower and
the tide of Greeks already erasing the shoreline.

The roads swerving up through the foothills like fingers traced
through sand.

Whereas with him he brings
the little son covering his ears.

A single tall stem extends skyward, its head bursting into white.

They still want the machine images to confirm:
the eggs keep falling inside.

The question is whether I am the jackrabbit taking in
the morning shade through her ears
or the trees frantically waving their bloated hands around her,
lacing their seeds into the ground with prayer.

Things are different if you are always in sunglasses,
like darker but more bearable.

California dumb with its glass buildings pressing their noses against
     each other.
California the vinyl flooring over the ground already drained.

When Aeneas was drawn out from the city walls
he went
to preserve his line.

To what end? The child's feet held
always to the fire.

On the highway due east, the tumbleweed lopes.
There is no future here. I've told you this before.

Fanfare for the Dinosaurs, or, The Trumpeter

Agnes Martin, Untitled (Innocence)

As if I had done a thing to deserve it—this delight
       —the afternoon air is
filled, not only with the usual clatter of mountain spring
          —the paving trucks dragging
     their stomachs along the newly-milled curb like seals heading
  up

the beach, the nickel hail flipping across the aluminum
       porch's broad sun hat—but
with the blowing of a young trumpeter who, by afternoon,
         has already worn right through
     someone in the house and finds herself rehearsing in the yard.

Nothing is ejected from my walls—not railroad spikes, antlers
      found prone, stone fragments printed
with fossilized ferns. For Agnes, innocence is six pale bars.
        She is always wearing stripes,
     which leads one to wonder whether the work influenced the
  shirts

or the other way around. The one woman in the English royal
    trumpeting
      corps wears a coat resembling
a pile of rugs. Some things are not worth it. The trumpet has no
        particular location
     to speak of—not like the next-door Post-it entreating us

to *please return the rake*. She takes us all with her into the
     air. She knows three entire
songs. One is a fanfare. I am hoping it provides a general good, as it
       has already done for me.
     Not far from here is a hillside where people figured out that
  standing between two

rocks could project their sounds in a perfect acoustic balance,
                suggesting, as we like to
believe, that things were made with our weird little voices in mind,
                    and just below are the foot-
           prints of dinosaurs who hiked straight up the hill's face. Touching them

did not make them seem more real. They remained, in my mind, like some-
                thing printed from a textbook
image, too precise with their curving toes to be so antique.
                    The trumpeter forever
           returns to her calling card—the theme from *Jurassic Park.*

This is not an adventure park, unless you count the ducks who
                like to leave their enclosure
and take to the sidewalk in protest. They are insecure or
                  unsecured. The trumpeter,
           maybe, is seeding us all with little bulbs of rebellion,

the music entering our habits like misplaced grenades. A
                balloon you've forgotten that
pops at the top of the staircase in the night. No one's measured
                  stripes fall outside the range of
           the comets. The white horse, the trumpet are just the first
      signs.

Easter Observance in which My Wife Has Misplaced Her Glasses Again

Eagle Rock, California

A place defined by shadow, as when,
at certain times of day, the outcrop of rock

spills a pool of darkness beneath its lip:
the descending shape of the eagle across stone.

Trail— a strong word for the sequence
of switchbacks between cacti on the slopes,

the expansive views of the 134. I admit
to liking freeway cars following their course

precisely like zippers pulled from the east,
the bridge holding off its own buckle.

Where I walk, a gauntlet of yellow flowers
swats against my shins. One blossom

attaches itself to the loop of my boot laces,
and I leave it be. When I was small, one

ritual I loved was flowering the cross.
The morning of the resurrection, each

picked a few sprigs of fresh blooms
and before entering the service placed

them on a chicken-wire cross at the door.
The children carried the structure in

procession down the aisle, a trail of tulips
in their wake. When springtime runs

empty, we put something new in its place.
Now, I am hiking on Easter. At the peak,

two plastic chairs with broken backs:
not so heavy, but awkward to haul up

the dry-grooved trail above the canyon.
During the walk, the eagle stretches larger.

How did the first people know, in the sunlight,
what was descending here—the eagle,

an angel, a shape too shifty for geometry?
In this moment I wish for her presence

and vision—the difference between eagles
adult and juvenile easy for her to spot,

as when the birds flew over the frozen
sand at Bishop's Beach and sat in their ring

around the tectonic rims of the dumpsters.
She never has her glasses. *Let me borrow yours,*

she said, already reaching for my face.
For a moment, my vision was short—just

extending to her pupils as they followed
the swooping birds, full-feathered and

kinetic in her eyes. A place defined
by shadow—and by the entering light.

THINE

Theory of Engagement

In these hypotheticals, something is pointed right at you but won't
    ever land.

She is always singing that song about the moon watching. It wasn't
    meant to be a lullaby, but that's how she's using it.

The tomatoes are world-famous, depending on what world you're
    living in.

Like the peacock throwing out its feathers. Nobody knows what to do
    with extremes.

The last owners took everything except the portraits of Jesus in every
    room.

In an effort to transmit his energy to the children, he would throw his
    baton into the woodwinds, where it would clatter down through
    the rickety stands.

It's not the same as performing. More akin to rapture.

He poured gasoline on the trash pile in the field nearest the house and
    lit it.

You'll take your eye out.

And then what to do with it.

Missiles and people all move the same on maps, in arrows.

The soil is changed forever. Half-lives and all that.

You can do nothing or confront. You can lay out your choices on a
little table.

She's covering her eyes again to sleep.

I don't care much for the racing, but I do like walking through the
stables as the horses all get dressed.

The crickets either mean everything's fine or it's not.

My job in the clock tower building was to call people and renew their
life insurance. They always asked me if something was wrong,
as if I'd know.

Out in the fields at night, that's when you'd see a ghost.

Just the one, leaning up against the shed like a potato sack.

The bullets come up in the swamp. Everybody stole them, but I wasn't
one of those kids.

Is anything approaching, or is it just the language coming at us.

He rented a log-splitter out at the river that kept catching fire.

There's no sense being too specific about the kneeling to be done.

The Fish

The mustachioed fish mow their lips / across the water's upper rim

in gulps optimistic and broad / like the first two bites in the pie-eating

race before everyone wishes their / hands were not tied at their backs.

The fish all group by the footbridge / as though to see me, so polite

but a bit overwhelming: all / their hip swivels and expectant eyes

and I am such a bad dancer. / But unlike them I can take in the air

without really feeling full, unless, / I mean, I want it—to blow a long,

loud wobbler through one of those / tubes we teach children to play,

to sink myself in a lap pool and glide, / arms arrow-strict to the other wall.

Do the fish feel that bursting? / There were too many people

jostling for a photo in front of / the bridge, the kind we think suitable

for special occasions. They did not care / for the presence of fish or for me

and it was clear in their camera angles. / They did care about leaving their feet

on the ground, and you can see / why. We are cranky when wet.

The fish open their eyes with the same / shock each time they breach surface.

Then back to the gallant backdrop of stone. / Do you remember the opera

company all in black, the one red star / coughing blood redundantly
    on herself?

Each of these fish has some bite of red / in its costume. Along the path, I trill

my fingernails along sheaths of bamboo, / which shade their own pipes,

throw a parachute of shade. / Each stem releases that little hum

of its own. A sign precedes the forest: / *Do Not Write on the Bamboo.*

Self-Portrait as Cain and Abel
after Jorie Graham

1

On the way to the field, one brother's step

2

a little too light, the other's burdened.
How does sin wait at the tent flap?
In a rough squat, ready to seize

3

or with its feet up, tapping its cigarette ash
into the soil. There are many ways

4

to wait, one brother thought, selecting

5

the place. There are many ways to give,
thought the other, eyes lingering along
the low stone wall marking the path.

6

The problem was too loud too quiet too nervous too presumptive.
One saw it in the other's boots. The other saw it in the sheep
bleating reliably. They were good-looking sheep,

7

fluffy and so on. Can one really be blamed

8

because the earth bears hard and rude forms?

9

Warted squash, carrots like elongated toes, the settling weight of pears.
Oh, they are beautiful, too. Among the most.

10

But might He not have needed a respite from the politics of fruit?

11

The sheep stood scattered in the field, repeating their little shouts.
Was it spring, with the miniatures standing beside their mothers
magnetically? Perhaps they had already gone off

12

in search of whatever else there is. The brothers
have almost reached the field.

Ars Poetica with Goats and Agnes Martin

When my friend asks me to describe the routes
through the park, I explain the first path

around the lake, the peripheral shrubs and ferns,
each plant tagged neatly with origin. Along

the second route, the gardens slip, as though
at dusk, through the quiet groves at the edge

of the farm, meadows bisecting the continents
of flowers. One garden, still in its corset.

The second, the poem in which my friend
raised the pigs in the meadow by hand, nursing

from bottles and teaching commands I thought
reserved for dogs or exceptional cats.

In the drawing of another landscape, I see
an order like intention in the generation of forms,

the wavering free hand revealed in the graphite
grid. The point is error, the absence or presence

of the pigs, a geography of the gradual.
The beauty is fault. Over this hill, the orchard

where apples still loosen the hems of the trees
and geese practice their angle. Remember,

there is precedent for everything. Jacob worked
for seven years and he received a wife, although

not the one he wanted. In this poem, I wish each
blossom gathering its bed, each bed overlaid

in the garden. The silhouette of the goats
at the fence for a handful of pellets as evening falls,

their cries too littered with grunts to mark
on a staff, but sketching their own rough pattern.

Rubicon

I found myself on a dock
overlooking
      the river longer

      than the eye.
A monarch

tapped its wings along
      the reeds
and left. Along

the banks, a parking
      lot full
with empty

trailers whose boats had already
      cast off
and now, indeed,

      were little
flecks in the eye, drifting

across its horizon like waiting
on the stoop
for anyone

on a summer evening.
      You saw
them waving down

from their sleeping
porches. Taking the air.

The way they layered on
        one another
        across the houses

and never came down.
All their cans
        so cold.

The river has met me
here and

we've neither brought
        something to say.
Did you know, anyway,

that the river
        is not so wide. A few steps,
and you're on
the other side.

Tell me what I can't uncross.
        The single lens
flare of the garage

light. The roads still
        closed through
the mountains in summer

snow, the warning gate bearing
        down its simple arm.

The worst chess player, I
          never calculate
my opening gambit.

The moth comes
          again and again to plead
its whole body

          against the screen door.
Nothing is
          here until the light

has pressed its hands
          against the face.

The yard, from darkness, springs
          up along the wall:

the walk,
          the grass, the patio

with its geometric rug
          angling through the chair
legs.
          In the desert,

the radio instruction on bird calls
          the only signal. On the banks,
it was not Caesar

himself but some guy with
          a stolen trumpet
who crossed first.

A new template.
           In the night,
the baby screams

           and in the morning
has forgotten it all.
That kind of washing away.

Two

THINE

Eve from Above

Enter dipping close
to the mountains, the sheep bouldering
            their positions along
the ridge. As long

as you can feel the air
pressing against the mere

            glass and engine rattle,
the mountains must be
on one side, the valley on the other.

Or else the image dies.
Or else the brush and purple flowers
            draw higher

breath while the evergreens wait below.

What does it mean to be patient?
Even the needles clinging on in
            the breeze will let
go. Or the plant which, once
                        trod, takes one

hundred years to
            reproduce its
head. A woman walks
            the tree

line, tracing it with her body, and down
   to the rocky
   bed of fish
in spread formation, and back again

to the flowers purpled
   by closeness
to the sun. The hillside does not end,
always pushing the outside

   world up and down
   on its shoulders.
Connecting, again, earth and sky.

I guess this is the time when everyone arrives.

The flowers grow as if they cannot
see themselves. The fish

   after an origin
that is not seeking them.
You, watching, are like the paws

reaching at them from above,
muffled by the evening river's roll;

you, watching, are like
   the rocks shaken loose
   from their beds,
a swifter rain. A face above, just

outlining its own moon.
   Braided river pulled strand
by strand from its riverbank

husk. When the woman
        bends into a drink of water
from the stream, the mosquitos fill

her mouth. She cannot let them out.
        She will.

California

and when the hills opened
a canyon in the crook of
one arm   we all ran in
carrying the road between us

like a carpet   like a casket
we placed it in the lowest
fold of the valley and set
the houses smart at its sides

the canyon was already
grinding in its sleep and
to use the self as a barrier
is a great act of bravery

in our culture   even if
one's position is fault
in any case   words come
down faster from mountains

where we render ourselves
with baskets grammatically
open for the next season of fires
to paint us in ash once again

A Suitable Host

September, I am expanding in all
sorts of ways, surprising only
because I am not prone to belief
in the apps that foretold what was
coming: the baby sized like an apple
then butternut squash; a tomato and
a postcard in the same week. Equivalence
requires imagination. Now two
buttons barely keep their heads
afloat above the baby's stretch inside.
At the cabin, I leaned my arms on
the scrappy porch table, which for some
time had not discharged its splinters
and found me a new and suitable host.
A problem is not better if you can see it.
I knew each time the fire alarm shrieked
in the night exactly what its trouble was,
but I could not find the right combination
of long and short prods with the broom
handle to calm it. Nothing was aflame.
It was just being a fucker, as I explained
to my stomach. The world is full of them.
I was trying to make good choices, so I
did not build a tower of chairs and books
and suitcases to try to reach the alarm
way up in the peak of the cabin ceiling,
but I did fantasize about it in detail for
nearly two hours in the intervals, ten
minutes between cries, until somehow
it acquiesced. The morning was beginning
again; I went in my thick coat to the rise

above the playa where I could watch
the sun drifting out over the sand. Where
the phone received just enough input that
I could be sure I was still there, at the end
of the messages. Across the open field,
the clustered deer headed down a different
path. The whites of their tails barely
signaled their departure into dawn.

Theory of Recitation

Like you're singing, the Latin
      teacher said of our chant, in the new
room without windows

      to shoot into. At home, I hummed
the assigned lines again asking
      for the causes of celestial

anger that drove the man from
      Trojan shores. Fear is not
the province of any particular time:

      the rash of baby-snatchings, or
the idea of one, around my birth. Police
      horses in their pen beneath

the highway trusses, our eyes up
      to their chests. The swamp into
which we were sinking but refused

      to look at our feet. Ask Sybil:
Until you have prayed the great
      mouths of my house are dumb

and will not open. Instead we saw
      the film in which a red-furred devil
lures students to their deaths, one

      by one, in a high school's dark wing.
The novels in which everyone
      disappears over breakfast, but you.

At long last you have done with the perils
        of the ocean, but worse things remain
for you to bear on land. Two women

        supervise from a tent beside Salvation
Mountain, where paint piled
        thirty years obscures the previous

revelations. The message
        arranged and dry like two wings
pinned apart on a corkboard:

        Say Jesus I'm a Sinner takes top.
The woman just beyond
        the mountain, whose long white

garment absorbs the desert's red
        swirl before it reaches the face.
The child raptured in its folds.

Pause One Coast

Is it the people or the land
the land or the people
the peopled land the landed people

The lawyer says a baby in the city is yours

      One coast rolling in at us pauses

When you cross into the mountains
no one keeps

even the hairs of their head
from the wind

Desert Meeting

On the spined arms of Joshua trees, the night
birds flip their side to side heads like bolts.
The panel of sky lit as though by one stray
beam through cracked curtains. When Yael drove
the tent peg through the temple of the general's body—
did it matter what happened before, now that it was
done? The tent saw everything. It always does.
We pass back and forth across desert as simply
as a lemon changing hands. Each memory a hard
stone's throw across the water, to prove you've still
got an arm. The tent rounds over us as (somewhere)
the forest drapes rain on its back. Bags double-zipped,
we light the little match again, which has nowhere
to go, which can only serve to bring the tent down.

Theory of Paradise

The purpose of the grooves is that cows will not pass over them, no matter
what.

As long as one foot remains touching, time can move in any direction it wants.

The bicycle on the platform circled by easels. Each body around sketching
its form in continuous loops.

To be itinerant does not stand in opposition to home, but in propulsion of it.

In Sarah's living room, we shared the finger puppets: boils, locusts, blood,
firstborn.

As if, by tracing the outline of the bicycle again and again, it would begin to
contain itself.

I could no longer run between the rows of corn without knocking them with
my shoulders.

To exit the point of origin presses the narrative to time. An initial stitch.

At birthday parties, children also ate the dog food, but in quantities of daring.
We were not yet domestic or thoroughly watched.

The plagues destroyed all systems of keeping time: the sun, the harvest,
the long, bent line of childhood.

Whether the garden was part of the farm, or just the kitchen extending its desire into the yard.

I liked the little rings that held tight around the cows' right ears.

At precisely 11:30, the sun enters the driveway over the canyon walls. So we need the umbrellas for the picnic.

Time as the bare floor on which we trace each shadow over the existing tiles.

We should get a bigger bed, she says, although the closet door already jams against the one here.

The cows stood around the lake, swatting the disinterest from their backs.

What prevented them from entering the garden again, other than language?

The horse tumbles forward in each of the quick-flipped photos. He cannot shift the frame, although somehow it moves to contain him.

Old Dominion

You are always astonished by what you already know:
the woodpile snake, the bridge whose scalp remains hinged
in place even when the fog sifts through its hair. I refuse
to say I know the baby inside until she kicks me. We operate

on these evident truths—if the diner is paper-walled with
scripture, we are not two queers between Matthew and John.
This morning I caught a big spider in a jar as he made his way
through the kitchen, and, for now, I've left the jar outside

with him. It's an unfair burden on his release, figuring
out what to do with it now. There's the man who parks
his truck each morning on the main drag and leaves it,
one window cracked so you can slip in your cash—

the prices all marked on the coolers in the bed: crabs, oysters.
Till they run out. I think, of all the lives, the woodpile
snake is a nice one—he is permitted in company, when polite;
he has a little cove where the wind stays off his back when he

comes in from winding through the rushes or playing
cards or whatever he gets up to. When anything changes
for him, it comes quick—the river in autumn rising fast
against his belly, the one glint of shovel before the snap.

[Willa to Edith]

Sunday

I am   looking out

                    forgotten

                              saturated

                                        in   moonlight.

            out of your   sight

        in the West;

                                                              the clear rose

                    unfailing
                        and horrible

[Willa to Edith]

    tuck

          in

            for sleep

         clear mountain

                      it's

unparalleled—

                  the zenith

        in a   day
         the sun gone down

                                   reminds one of

   that beauty,
             mathematics

       you

                                wait

[Willa to Edith]

the Lady   slips down

about 8:30

fated and unfailing

because we can

I have   almost constantly

carried

time

Theory of Communion

From the second row of bar stools in the balcony, the long look down
        to the stage
where three women play their guitars in garland
                crowns handed up from the crowd.

If you could trace the lines of sight from each person suspended
                through the room
       and see their ends
knot neatly on the center mic stand, draped in holiday lights.

Not present is someone who could calculate the total number
                  of air particles in this room.

This is a body this is a body this is a body.

        Always on land and envious of
the ducks who stick their heads down into the lake and see the kingdom.

The preservationists breathe their stiffening air onto little squares of stopped
        time throughout the city.

If you can see the past, you aren't trapped in it yet.

Have you spent the evening around a big pile of dimly lit crabs.
             I hear a little bit of that in you.

    The pedal can make a loop with any sounds you want, but
eventually you will have to leave
    that pattern, break.

The ledge is outfitted with a little shelf because even holding
a drink too long is tedious to us.

The year of the supergroup is now.

As though you could lift the brittle buildings
with tweezers into metal-capped jars.

This is a body. This is a way to get up but what.

The supergroup appears
on stage in matching black jackets. One has a silver cut-out of Idaho
pinned to her back.

The wedding lawn at the top of the hill, a room's worth
of Astroturf layered over the sand.
Extraordinarily green, in the way that lies are.

To fix your wardrobe, pick a style icon: a famous person you collect
pictures of online.
In the evenings, you can break their outfits into pieces,
reconfigure them on top of yourself.

You have to break the body.

The pig roasting all night in the parking lot
for the barbecue. Tomato or vinegar
for the winning sauce.

Someone tells me that
my jacket is starting to look
a little tattered. But I don't want to change
it until my body stops moving around.

At ten, I drew city blocks, which I stored
on long sheets of paper
beneath my bed. Each an imagined radius that met only my needs.

If the time had come to assemble some of these parts—
the city, the body, the crowns—each into
a new place.

Who is the breaking for? Not you.

THINE

THREE

THINE

Self-Portrait as Woman with Horns

                                  Once I tried / measuring myself
                  by displacement.
A delicate labor
           to move from outline / to what
                 has been replaced. It / reminded me of how
           I learned to tuck my head / to chest when flipping
at the end of a lane—how once I was only
          a single fist leading / the way into a wall,
              a grape at the tongue's tip / preparing
                    for its mighty downward roll.

Vanitas

Did the painters need a real
        skull or had their lives been
so marked by graves they could
        do it from memory,
                how if buried too close

to the top layer in permafrost
        the bodies just push back
up. I have been thinking lately
        of Brian flat on his back
                across the tundra, reading

a novel the night before his team
        heads out to tag loons, the head-
lamp letters of the book
        in a little green pup tent
                pulling him outside

time while all the night sky
        holds an open door.
The wait the next day for
        the loons who, netted, weigh
                the sack of a hand-

held scale like a yolk
        slipping from an
egg. In the video online,
        an image guides: another
                team atop a lake nets

the birds, plops them one
        by one into a little buzzing
whaler. The loons,
        apprehended, turn
            to the tight flashlight

beam as it approaches, all
        eyes. Easier, the narrator
says, to tell the banded
        individuals from the
            common species.

What a narrow thing
        to be seen. I have
said as much in spring
        to the daffodils elbowing
            up again where grass

has tried to squat. For
        the loud arrival of everyone
who, once seen, will die.
        I don't make the rules.
            I've been wearing

overalls again, something
        to slip wholly into, like hearing
geese outside and opening
        the door to find
            they've already spilled

across the sky. In the house,
        someone sings to the baby,
"Sweet Caroline," at the table
        where on her birthday,
            the yellow Formica spread

with a dinosaur cloth, we
        followed in numbers the new
life. See, ourselves, all is not
        lost. All is quiet. We talk
           about them still: which had

short arms and fast legs,
        which cried, and which like
a gentle wave rolled grasses
        into their mouths, crushed
           between teeth, swallowed wide.

Invitation to an Evening

Dear ones, if at any time
        you have need of a beginning, look
toward that early summer evening
        on the hillslopes, just beyond
where we had pitched the diligent brown
        tent and engaged in roasting
vegetables in campfire

        foil when a deer also entered
across the footlights and began
        rummaging between campsites
for mouthfuls of grass.
        She came, took only a few
steps between each darling
        swallow, bent open-hinged to

every new scoop of grass floating
        improbably on the sandy ground,
supposing each as good as the next
        and as perfect. There was nothing
to do when the triangle of
        her face met the triangle of grass
but for one to collapse into

        the other. To turn the foil packs
onto their backs, keeping our eyes
        from the wind. Crossing
the threshold again and already, she
        went and returned having gathered
a friend, an alternate who preferred
        to remain curtained in the branches

of the one leafless tree and make
　　　　her meal in agreeable private.
Who is to say which deer is right?
　　　　As if to stress their perspectives,
the bold deer dispensed with her
　　　　role and backed herself down
like a gravel truck delivering a load,

　　　　a polite but visible few yards
away, which made me, I confess, as happy
　　　　as the spread of light char
over the packs of potatoes. It was
　　　　as though she had begun
a presentation with one of those
　　　　rubber-tipped pointing sticks,

explaining with relevant graphics
　　　　This Is My Body and Here
Is My Life. As though
　　　　we faced each other across
the burning-blue campfire and
　　　　asked *do you have need.* When
they departed, it was with

　　　　the understanding that only
so, in another location, could
　　　　we all arrive. We could say
come and see, some time, what is
　　　　beginning here. How we
are opening a little spark of time
　　　　and how it can be spent.

Whole Life

Miscalculating the date line, I arrived for my room
a day late, which was baffling to the clerk but seemed
            plausible to me.
That was yesterday, the clerk repeated. *I see that now,*

I said. Alone in London, I took to picnicking in the park
each evening with the free newspaper placed in hand, which I
            always accept: a system
to organize the time into cycles, as if one day

a single thing would change. Just down the path,
a half-mile or so, I wandered to the new installation
            in the boat pond:
thousands of oil barrels bound in a pyramid of eager purple

and pink. They were supposed to represent input or output
or something over time, the lake and sky here forming a new
            set of axes
hyphenated by birds, but I found them very loud after

a day with Lange's photos of women in deserts. Perhaps
I was in a mood that would not quantify. Perhaps I should
            have consulted
the chart that shows how geese convert into time. The exhibit

plaque had described *Lange's compulsion to crop in on the body.*
You can say a portrait is life-size, that it contains a whole life.
            Or that one
leash on free will is the frame. Lange went back later

to "Migrant Mother" and cut out a thumb, which means
one day, Lange (about her business, drinking coffee, whatever)
         thought: you
know what, off with that thumb. And it was hers to halve.

Mothering is the opposite of desert. In "Woman of
the High Plains," the grass expands the eye, settling into
         the deep well
of frame: a few fingers, a half-pour, the bare skin of sky

from which all problems emerge. Neck and forehead,
shadowed eyes, the rising proof of grass. Eventually, we all
         flee the drought.
In Coachella, Lange saw a carrot harvest where I saw windmills

measured perfectly from ground to sky. A crowd, machines
who here found their own. *You don't have to look. You
         can't help looking.*
Beneath Muybridge's horses, the trip wires prone across

the ground, each caught and yanked like bowstring to elicit
the camera's flash. The feet advancing their unsubtle arcs at
         each movement.
Then the moment when the horses have passed. *I tell you*

we weren't here yesterday. Another of your nightmares.
Is there any other way out of the frame? The baby waved at me
         from the pouch
on her father as we crossed the little stream into the turning

aspens. Her father, who said, *She does that all the time.*
She was wearing a fishing hat, like the men with their ankles
         in the stream.
My friend counts the fish on the river, says how many

taken, by whom. What makes a good run. The autumn light fit
me like an over-sized coat, unsure where to fold. I gave
      my days over
to counting, but only toward what would begin.

[Willa to Edith]

New

in your room,

I had
pleasure

a grand feeling

unparalleled

above the horizon

we are the only

Planets, dear,
— and they will   wait

[Willa to Edith]

My

     sitting   room

                                 has been

   the woods   in still   moonlight

    from now,   I shall

                           plan

  and

        fail

[Willa to Edith]

I wake up

                              in

           your window,
                shining

       a superb

    sun   behind Gap-mountain;

all that beauty, those

                      temperatures.

         next week

   I must dress

                     for

                    summer.

THINE

Landscape Beginning with a Line from Marianne Moore

You remember the Israelites who said, "If
only we had died in Egypt, or even here
in the wilderness!" They were not
standing on the bike path by the Santa
Fe River, as I am, bounded by lizards,
prairie dogs batting at thin leaves
like little punching bags before
gallantly swallowing each whole.
They run nearly parallel to the soil,
unaffected, it seems, by the sun,
the stubbornness of the old bicycle and
its slippery chain. A luxury to sit in
the sweaty foam seat of my own choices,
in which no one else is required to pool.
I have just come south from a summer
in which people were forever vanishing
into the woods holding tight around
the city, finding their own portals out
of this time. There's no purpose in
temperance, I said to myself, evenings
at the desk supporting my habitual
glass of red. Be scorched or be gone.
I rode the bicycle in the summer
afternoons with no hat, a radical hoping
to reveal my root. The prairie dogs
and I shared no concern for the coyotes
(unrevealed but promised *close at hand*),
the little ants in their skyscraping
humps, ample amongst the low brush,
prickly and broad. Like them, I prefer
to complain behind closed doors.

I had not come all that far, just beyond
the evenly-housed streets and across
the river bridges. I have not starved
for a little tendril of my own.

THINE

Taking Off My Eyes

By the lake, evergreens the color of all
      the backpacks in green—forest, kelly— needles
ripening from dark to light across each branch.
      Among the trees like legs like limbs
you wait while the breeze ripples
      one end of the lake, shaking crumbs
from the cloth that won't shake.

Isn't it exhausting to look, only to have
      everything change before the words catch
up, panting and disappointed;
      isn't it exhausting to keep running
toward the lake with words slipping
      from your palms anyway, falling into

the dirt. Like our stubborn effort to describe
      the doors of our house to visitors—*really yellow,*
we tell them, and they always arrive—*really*
      yellow, the cycle of the plant called, wonderfully,
"basket of gold," at the back door pushing out
      its blooms. What once was an orange
poppy did nothing to protect its suns

      from the baby's hands as she plucked
them petal by petal, and, satisfied, reversed
      course: placed each petal carefully back
onto the plant, weighting its leaves—always
      too big, too destructive in love. How
we scatter our evenly arranged bulbs

through the pine sprigs, cranberries on string,
        and think this is the world. The wind
licks the corner of the lake, from which, later,
        I will drink through the flimsy filter
straw, and already it will no longer be the lake
        I remember—rocks, grass floating in strands—
beneath us, clogged mirror as the continent divides.

Watch

I don't notice, for months,
the unmarked cars,
their hips to the curb along the street.

The house next door
from which no one seems to go
from walls, defined
in this case by a trellis of vines.

In that house, the governing
aesthetic is silence. Next
door, my house: a patio
on which someone reads
in a little palm forest. I do like it.

I have chairs, lights, a table
on which to spread a meal,
the big wooden door which I can open
and close as I please even on such a whim

as the movement of sunlight.
The company of traveling cats,
and the thin bulbed beads of light.
And so I am satisfied and believe my fortress
better than the others.

To surround is to *flow over,* from *super* and *undare:*
a concept to which walls exist as a challenge.
Accept no gifts,
keep thine enemies to the beach.

The Israelites walked in
silence around the walls of Jericho
for six days in spectral loops, prey

wrapped in their rope-like tail.
And the woman who lived in
the wall, who lowered the spies worm-like
from her windows—of course

the wall collapsed on the seventh day
with that kind of cavity.

They could not withstand the vision.

This seems the theory of the unmarked cars,
for months circling
around a crime unknown to us.

Their presence indicates an impending
collapse, if not
of the structure, of its inhabitants;

the grass left to its own heights, a thousand
flags of retreat.

Theory of Sand

Our voices in the dark across the improbable sand
hills sheathed in mountains. No flares. Red-beamed

headlamps and the tug of clouds, Venus in its brightest sequins
a little gaudy, the ridge holding us up across its spine. We

strummed it with our feet like strings. Nothing is too early except
in our expectation. We already knew blankness, had heard the song

of innocence—its high-pitched arc floating out of car windows
and across the meadow somewhere back East. I was dressed in black,

and for days the sand ran out from my toes. *There is no point in being any
more sensitive.* In one story, the stars twist above us like a lid clicking shut.

In another, we lie prone on the surface, for once not interfering,
as we wait for the house lights to dim, the curtain to rise.

To Autumn

The bear, as I came to know her,
liked dandelions. She liked to wander the edge
of the gravel inroad with a wiggling strut,

mowing blossoms into her
mouth, to nestle in one spot and chomp
through all within jaw's reach. She did not mind
observation, which has always been

a problem of mine
when eating. We stood on the slope,
an army installation on one side;
the other, a ski slope dormant, lift
cars still suspended.

Their circulation a feature of seasons,
strange and regular as the fall of snow
from the peaks to the valleys, then reversed.

Elisha was taunted by a horde of children
(42, in some accounts)
for his baldness as he walked along the road, which inspired him

to summon two bears
from God. Surely he was surprised by the volley
of children's voices, but was he by their insults?
No life escapes cruelty, even for prophets.

Bears gird themselves with the necessary
weight for the future: *hibernus,* adj.
for the qualities of winter. To be wintry
oneself, an entirely separate condition.

For a week, the whale sat
on the shore, already considered
by science, pronounced naturally dead.
Before the bears arrived, the city formed

a line, half a mile through shin-deep mud, to have a look.

He lay reclined, fins to the sides, as you might
any night, glasses still propped
across your nose; his body, improbably large and

ribbed like thick rubber. Surrounded by
pilgrims, he unfolded his skin into water around
us. His final form submerged in air.

It's a Day

in which we all are stretching our
harmlessness across the hours, shifting
at each ping to a new display. The aspen
is shaking again, but has calmed
from full-fledged tremors to a silent
pillar of waving hands—not the kind delighted
to find you here on the cabin porch, but
the sort that are not sure if they knew you
in the past. I had so adapted myself
to our silence that I forgot to make enough
noise while circling the lake and startled
not a bear, but a bush, which seemed to rev
itself into a roar nonetheless, quite like
the sound a few days earlier when my car
expired in a mouthful of its own
breath outside of Wendell, Idaho,
as though it knew that muscles expel
what remains at the end. Waiting for the tow,
I flipped through a magazine and the end
of a bag of sour gums that had found
its way to my person. The semi-trucks
recklessly flapped by. The bush was stuffed
with birds who, at my presence, flipped
their wings on all at once, as though
they had seen one of those walking
live nativities where, as you arrive,
the shepherds put down their juice boxes
and begin to sing off-key. When
the birds completed their individual
bursts outward, it was time to let them
re-set the scene: to move on to the next

section of narrative, which must exist
somewhere down the path trampled in
loose ends and roundabouts, one beginning
on which the needle descends again and again.

Poem Without Weight

You'll miss the
sense, in autumn,
        that something remains
to be lost, our desperate attempts
                to enumerate it.
The squirrel who, seeing

me, abandons
        the half-eaten
pumpkin fallen to our side

from the neighbor's yard.
        The leaves just so. In the warming
light of morning, the
        breeze through

                the old garage
where, on an old slab of wood and some
        boxes, I've made the writing

space. As quickly as I became
someone
        who felt hope, it drifted
out of reach. Maybe you can
        pinpoint

                the moment
you were the deer discovering
        its legs and seeing,
for the first
time, the meadow bound in trees.
        Both endless
and secure.

But think of all
            the times you have not been
that generous. The deer who runs.
            At night, leaving
the party, you couldn't make it
            back down
            the road without
stopping

under the wide-winged elm
            to kiss. And then,
like the pumpkin-glut squirrel,
            you were full

            beneath
the canopy of autumn leaves.
As though you'd seen
            the meadow, but not yet
the trees.
            Each blade of grass
intricate and sweet.

The Lightning Field, Walter De Maria

What's left for us
as we putter
            around the cabin
trying to get the proportion
            of coffee beans to water
in the old pot
right, trying

to get the language
        to press onto anything for more
        than a few instants, but it falls
like the figures
of prophets
always

        too weighty to stand
against the felt
board for their scenes.
        The field in which the propositions

jut to the sky, like hands
        expose their empty palms.
Click. The sky faints orange.
        Click. Dawn.

It's better to wait
        at the precipice:
as in the desert
at sunset, when the chill
        emerges from the ground, and
all you found rich
        and blooming
        and red
disappears
        with a cold shudder.

Whiskey full, you throw
        the light back in.
        As though every day
we practice,
        a little, the ending,
never knowing when someone will

risk the front steps and closed door
to collect. A long time,

                       you have not been
         one of the poles, solitary
in a crowd—but twinned,
         and now

              perhaps the whole
gridded field across which the dance
         leaves its tracks.

The birds never quieter than
today. Morning traffic
patterns light
         up, then wade
back out through the afternoons.
Like water spilled,

overflown
         error around
         all of our ankles. And very
low-cut socks. In the morning
         yard, the dead crow lay

perfectly between the blades
         of grass extending its wings.
              This once, thankful
that you had not
         mowed, that the grass
was softer

around. What am I supposed
         to want? To live alight
until falling straight

from the sky? More like
me, the cricket who,
across the concrete, drags a leaf
along in its legs.

The little garage along
the alley
that takes in the light
with the door
flung up
and its mouth exposed.

The workbench where I can lay
my tools
out, having built
what I can.

Strophe & Anti-Strophe

1.

Walking around the lake, I can't recall
        if Horace said poems should be
        sweet and useless or useful
and sweet. This distinction doesn't matter
        to the one who greets everything
        by saying *oh!* like she is trapped
somewhere in an ecstatic ode and *oh!*

        it all keeps coming. All around
        the buildings arch up in front
of the clouds, intercepting their patterns
        in glass. The homing geese proud to
        impose themselves a bit on
the lake. The trouble with you is that you

2.

Find too many things ripe: the opening
        of subway doors inviting
        you in. And yet, what use have you
to offer? At best, you are the squirrel
        holding fast to the center
        of the path and never giving

way. The world still rumbles above on its
        higher wheels. Let it be, when
        you pass through, that afterward your
weight remains: as when the horse has snorted
        the apple from your palm, now
        slick with spit—with its wild and rapt-
urous tongue, licked quivering red lips clean.

Notes

"Theory of Audacity" refers to Federico Barocci's painting *Aeneas Fleeing from Troy*.

"Fanfare for the Dinosaurs, or, The Trumpeter" comes from Agnes Martin's painting *Untitled (Innocence)*, which is at the Harwood Museum of Art in Taos, and the film *Agnes Martin: With My Back to the World* (2007), directed by Mary Lance.

"Theory of Engagement" takes after C.D. Wright's *Deepstep Come Shining*, including the paraphrased "You'll take your eye out. And then what to do with it."

"The Fish" was written for a call-and-response project edited by Sean Pears at *ythm*. The poem responds to Sally Keith's "The Garden Through Which We Have Walked Already."

"Self Portrait as Cain and Abel" borrows in its form from Jorie Graham's *The End of Beauty*.

"Theory of Recitation" draws on Leonard Knight's installation *Salvation Mountain* in Imperial County, CA; it also includes lines from David West's translation of Virgil's *Aeneid*.

"Whole Life" responds to Christo and Jeanne-Claude's *The London Mastaba* and *Dorothea Lange: Politics of Seeing* at the Barbican. Also, Eadweard Muybridge's experiments at Stanford and several italicized lines from *Waiting for Godot*.

The six poems titled "[Willa to Edith]" erase the one preserved letter from Willa Cather to her partner Edith. The letter can be found through the NET Foundation's *Yours, Willa Cather*, along with context provided by Andy Jewell.

"Self-Portrait as Woman with Horns" responds to Nicholas Kahn and Richard Selesnick's photograph *Melora*, and to the Denver Art Museum's *Stampede* exhibition.

"Invitation to an Evening" contains several slant-translated lines from Anton Chekhov's *The Seagull*.

"Landscape Beginning with a Line from Marianne Moore" includes italicized language from Marianne Moore's poem "Feed Me, Also, River God."

"Theory of Sand" uses italicized text from Adam Hadhazy's BBC Future article "What are the limits of human vision?" 27th July 2015

"Poem Without Weight" responds to Walter De Maria's Land Art installation *The Lightning Field* in New Mexico, and I am grateful to the Dia Art Foundation for the opportunity to visit.

The line misremembered in "Strophe & Anti-Strophe" from Horace's *Ars Poetica* is, in fact, line 343: "omne tulit punctum qui miscuit utile dulci," which, in the Poetry Foundation's translation, means "the writer who mixes the useful with the sweet carries the whole vote."

Acknowledgments

Poems in this manuscript have appeared, in these forms and earlier iterations, in the following journals:

Alaska Quarterly Review, "Self-Portrait as Cain and Abel"
The Collagist, "California"
Denver Quarterly, five "[Willa to Edith]" poems
DIAGRAM, "Theory of Engagement" and "Pause One Coast"
FIELD, "Fanfare for the Dinosaurs, or, The Trumpeter"
Jellyfish, "It's a Day" and "A Suitable Host"
Matter, "Desert Meeting" and "Landscape Beginning with a Line from Marianne Moore"
Michigan Quarterly Review, "Eve from Above"
Mid-American Review: "Invitation to an Evening" and "Old Dominion"
New South, "Strophe & Anti-Strophe"
Quarterly West, "Theory of Audacity"
River Styx, "Rubicon"
Seneca Review, "Self-Portrait as Woman with Horns"
Third Coast, "Ars Poetica with Goats and Agnes Martin"
Yale Review, "Ode on Inheritance"
ythm, "The Fish"

I am deeply grateful to the many people who supported me through every stage of writing this book. Thank you to my colleagues in both the Departments of English and Gender and Sexuality Studies at the University of Southern California for their feedback and encouragement. Thank you especially to the members of my dissertation committee, David St. John, Mark Irwin, Susan McCabe, John Carlos Rowe, and Ange-Marie Hancock Alfaro, for their time and guidance, and to Anna Journey, Carol Muske-Dukes, Janalynn Bliss, and Sandra Garcia-Myers for their essential advice and support.

Thank you to the USC Graduate School for providing me with time for writing through the Dornsife Graduate School Fellowship, the Research

Enhancement Fellowship, and the Summer Research and Writing Grant. I am also grateful to the Creative Writing Ph.D. program for support through summer writing and travel grants, and to Mr. and Mrs. Abbott Brown for the Maddocks-Brown Award for Contemporary Poetry. My sincere thanks, also, to the Santa Fe Art Institute and PLAYA for offering time and space to write.

Finally, I am grateful to my family and friends for their encouragement and patience. Thank you to Samantha Dextor and everyone at Tiny Hearts Academy, without whom this work would have been impossible. Thank you to Heather Adams, Kristen Bauman, Mariah Bauman, Mark Bruhn, Olena Kalytiak Davis, Scott Dimovitz, Nina Elder, Graham Faust, Sabrina Garcia, Amy Hezel, David Hicks, Chris Jacobs, Shizhen Jia, L.A. Johnson, Elizabeth Deanna Morris Lakes, Sarah Marcus, Siwar Masannat, Frank McGill, Hannah Miller, Lara Narcisi, Rich Neal, Cris Nunez, Daryl Palmer, Jeremy Pataky, Deb Preston, Amy Reitnouer, Callie Siskel, Olivia Tracy, Brian Uher-Koch, Michael Joseph Walsh, Erin Winterrowd, Neil and Julia Partridge, and all of my teachers. Finally, but certainly not least, thank you to Alyse Knorr and Lucy Knorr-Partridge for their unending generosity and good humor.

Kate Partridge

Kate Partridge is the author of one previous collection of poetry, *Ends of the Earth.* Her poems have appeared in *FIELD, Yale Review, Pleiades, Michigan Quarterly Review, Alaska Quarterly Review, Copper Nickel,* and other journals. A graduate of the MFA program at George Mason University and the PhD at the University of Southern California, she lives in Denver and teaches at Regis University.

Printed in the USA
CPSIA information can be obtained
at www.ICGtesting.com
JSHW082051290723
45531JS00002B/16